IMAGES
of America
WORLD WAR II
CHICAGO

The *Chicago Sun*, founded December 4, 1941, came into being because President Franklin D. Roosevelt had encouraged Marshall Field III to establish a paper to oppose Col. Robert McCormick's *Chicago Tribune*, which opposed American intervention into World War II. Three days after its founding, Pearl Harbor was bombed by Japan on December 7, 1941. This August 9, 1942 issue described and pictured U.S. infantrymen, armored divisions, artillery units and uniforms, insignias, and medals of honor given to American servicemen. In 1948, because of a merger, it became the *Chicago Sun-Times*.

IMAGES
of America
WORLD WAR II
CHICAGO

Paul M. Green and Melvin G. Holli

ARCADIA

Published by Arcadia Publishing,
an imprint of Tempus Publishing, Inc.
Charleston SC, Chicago, Portsmouth NH,
San Francisco

Printed in Great Britain.

Library of Congress Catalog Card Number: 2003112723

For all general information contact Arcadia Publishing at:
Telephone 843-853-2070
Fax 843-853-0044
E-Mail sales@arcadiapublishing.com
For customer service and orders:
Toll-Free 1-888-313-2665

Visit us on the internet at http://www.arcadiapublishing.com

Dedicated to Robert H. Green—
a brave young man.

CONTENTS

ACKNOWLEDGMENTS

We acknowledge assistance, research information, and photo use from the *Chicago Sun-Times* (especially John Cruikshank and Ron Theel), the City of Chicago, the University of Illinois at Chicago, Roosevelt University, the Civil Defense Committee, the Great Lakes Regional Federal Archives Center, the Martin Kennelly Collection, Saul Alinsky, Jane Addams, Urban Historical Collections, the Municipal Reference Library, and the Chicago Historical Society.

FOREWORD

Chicago: 1900–1941

Major American cities in the 18th and 19th centuries developed at "strategic breaks" in the line of transportation or trade such as where water transport was transferred to land transport; ocean transport to river transport; river to canal transport or Great Lakes shipping. The transportation revolution prodded by steamboats and canal building contributed to the growth of cities located at these breaks in the line of trade as was the case for Chicago. Chicago as an important transfer point for lake boats, steamboats, riverboats, canal barges, and later as the railroad center of mid-America grew enormously as a commercial city. Chicago as a transport center tapped the Midwest hinterlands for forest farm, animal ranch, and mine export production, and became an exchange point of manufactured goods for farm products. By 1900, Chicago had become a leading commercial city and the Midwest's railroad center.

A second factor in explaining urban growth was the industrialization of big cities when manufacturing moved from waterpower sites, often located near small towns, to steam power sites like Chicago. Chicago's lack of river rapids or falling water had delayed the growth of manufacturing until steam power boomed in the period after 1870 and electric power after the turn of the century. Cities that had been primarily commercial cities and transport centers evolved into commercial and manufacturing centers by 1900.

The history of modern urban growth of cities such as Chicago also has a strong link to the industrialization process. The Chicago connection is that Henry Ford, the father of assembly line manufacturing and mass production, claims to have gotten his idea from watching the Chicago meat packers "disassembly" line where the work came to the worker on an overhead pulley line and each slaughter house worker specialized in butchering one part of the beef or pork carcass. The assembly line system, which Ford perfected in Detroit in 1913 stressed that the worker was not to go to the work, but the work was to come to the worker waist high on a moving conveyor belt, and each employee became a specialist focusing on one part of the assembly process, as had been the case in the Chicago butcher trade. The Ford assembly lines enormously cut production time in motor vehicle manufacturing from days to hours and it also led to cost cutting by 85% from 1910 to the mid-1920s. The assembly line manufacturing mass production process would also expand in Chicago.

Mass production is also the principle of production for the masses. Mass production would lead to mass markets and the booming growth of the consumer society by the 1920s by which Chicago and American workers would be identified as the highest paid in the world. These large-scale markets made possible lower profit margins per unit, but an overall growth in the gross profits for the manufacturers and businesses by a principle called the "economies of scale." Manufacturing also located in growing cities such as Chicago because urban centers could provide the capital for investing that manufacturers needed, they were main centers for the flow of new immigrant populations that met the labor needs of factories and service industries, and large metropolitan areas such as Chicago also provided densely populated centers and public markets for sales at home as well as, in Chicago's case, a central transport center for shipping goods to the rest of the nation. European immigrants and rural Americans flocked to cities such as Chicago seeking and finding better paying jobs.

The economic triumph of urban industrialism was also accompanied by the expansion of city bound culture over the folkways of villages, farms, and rural residencies. By the turn of the century, the farmer was no longer considered the "noble son of the soil," but often derided as a "hayseed, a bumpkin or a rube" by urban commentators. The nation also began developing urban modes of dress, living, speaking, and entertainment culture. Standardized production and the expansion of the mail-order catalog businesses, which accelerated in Chicago companies such as Sears and Roebuck, contributed to the standardization of clothing styles, culture, and other styles of life in rural and immigrant America.

Urban journalism was also a powerful force in spreading the gospel of urbanization. Drab metropolitan newspapers of the 1870s were transformed into sensational "yellow journalism" in the 1890s, which carried over into the 20th century and which featured sensationalism, cartoons, simplistic writing styles, and large print pictures, which appealed to non-English speaking as well as semi-literate urbanites from abroad as well as the countryside. Cities also developed an increasing grip on the artistic and literary community in America, which had not been the case in the 19th century. For example, the literary "transcendental movement" of the middle third of the 19th century featured writers such as Ralph W. Emerson, Henry D. Thoreau, and Nathaniel Hawthorne who came from rural America and celebrated life in small town and rural America. By the late 19th and early 20th centuries, America's literary focus was shifting to cities such as Chicago where novelists such as Theodore Dreiser and Frank Norris, along with poets like Carl Sandburg wrote about urban topics and captured the national literary interest. The Chicago metro area has also become the home of famous architects such as Louis Sullivan, Dankmar Adler, and Frank Lloyd Wright.

A large European migration had helped Chicago's population double almost every decade since the end of the Civil War. Before then, most of the migrants had come from Ireland, Germany, and England. After 1870 southern, eastern, and central Europeans flocked to Chicago—including Italians, Greeks, Poles, Russian Jews, Ukrainians, and Bohemians, along with Dutchmen and Scandinavians. By 1900, out of Chicago's 1.7 million population, some 587,000 were foreign born and another 728,000 were native born of foreign-born parents.

Chicago had become a very ethnic city. The famine-fled Irish had come as Anglophobes, with a love of Ireland and their Catholic religion as an important spiritual as well as cultural resource. Beginning as humble canal diggers and laborers, the children of these Emerald Islanders soon came to dominate the "Irish trinity" of American urban life: the priesthood, the police, and politics. Every Catholic bishop from 1847 to 1916, with one exception, was of Irish ancestry. The Chicago police force was disproportionately Irish by the turn of the century and would remain so for the rest of the century. All but two of Chicago's publicly elected mayors since 1933 have been of Irish Catholic heritage.

Chicago's German immigrants, who by 1910 were the city's largest ethnic group, had also influenced the cultural and economic development of the city. Many who had come were skilled immigrant coppersmiths, tin smiths, iron molders, and carpenters, who were all an important part of the labor force that was rebuilding Chicago after the Great Fire of 1871, and who also helped the industrial development of the city. The Chicago Symphony Orchestra was founded in 1891 by German-born conductor Theodore Thomas, who played a major role in bringing European classical music into Chicago's cultural market place. They were also the nation's first ethnic war victims when America went to war against their homeland in 1917 and again in 1941, which sped up their Americanization.

Although fewer in number than the Germans, Chicago's Swedes were drawn to residential areas and occupations similar to those of the Germans. Although poor when they got off the boat, these migrants were primarily Lutheran and middle-class in ethos and outlook and were among the first of the 19th century immigrants to Chicago to begin to move to less densely populated areas of the city and to the suburbs.

Chicago's Jewish population was drawn from two different national regions of Europe. German Jews had come in the 19th century and were already successful as a business class by the turn of the century as owners of large-scale corporations such as Hart Schaffner and Marx, Florsheim Shoes, Spiegel mail-order sales, and above all, Sears and Roebuck Company. The latter enterprise was taken over in 1908 and operated by German-Jew Julius Rosenwald. Rosenwald turned a small watch sales firm into a multi-million dollar mail-order corporation. It was said at the time that "Julius put the bucks into Sears and Roebuck." A successful businessman, Rosenwald was one of the wealthiest Chicagoans as shown by the first federal income tax figures in 1913. As a philanthropist, he donated millions for building black schools and also gave five million dollars to found the Museum of Science and Industry.

Julius Rosenwald also started the Hebrew Aid Society to help his poorer country cousins, Russian Jews, to acculturate and adjust to life in America and Chicago. Although they settled in a densely populated poor ghetto known as Maxwell Street, the second generation experienced success. Arthur Goldberg, a presidential cabinet member and Supreme Court justice, was the son of Joseph Goldberg, a peddler who was so poor that he could only afford to buy a blind horse to pull his cart. Samuel Paley, who became president of CBS broadcasting, was the son of a hole-in-the-wall cigar maker. Benny Goodman, the "king of swing" music by 1940, and Admiral Hyman Rickover, the father of the nuclear Navy, were the sons of poor immigrant tailors, and Barney Balban who later became the president of the Paramount Motion Picture Company was the son of a grocery store runner. One can conclude that poor Eastern European Jews moved into dirty slums and rundown ghettos when they arrived, but the slums did not hurt them, for many came out as nationally distinguished professionals and prosperous businessmen. By the 1920s, the prospering second generation was moving out of the slums into less densely populated areas of Chicago such as Lawndale and Douglas Park and thereafter to the North Side and the suburbs.

Other Eastern European immigrants such as Poles also left their homeland that was occupied by three imperial powers—Germany, Austro-Hungary, and Russia—and sought to keep their ethno-linguistic culture alive in America and cities such as Chicago. Since Poland did not exist as a nation, these Polish migrants sought to create a solid "Polonia," a nation within a nation in Chicago based on churches, building and loan associations, parochial schools, and fraternal associations. Catholicism was a key national identity for Polish-Americans, who also had the largest ethnic attendance figures for parochial Catholic schools. Another Czar and later Soviet occupied group that sought to keep its ethno-linguistic culture alive in America was Chicago's Ukrainians. They had also hoped to use the United States as a launching pad as had the Poles and Bohemians in World War I to win independence for their homeland, but the pendulum of history no longer swung to the tune of self-determination as it had under President Woodrow Wilson, whose pressures in the Versailles Peace treaty had won independence for two of the above mentioned nations.

Unlike the Poles, some immigrant groups such as Bohemians, Lithuanians, and Italians had a bigger split between religion and nationalism. Italian immigrants were often content to send their children to public schools instead of church schools and Bohemians, who were known for their anti-clerical and free-thought lodges, established a Bohemian National Cemetery to bury their free thinkers since the church refused them burial space. Many of Chicago's Italians were migrants from impoverished south Italy and Sicily who distrusted governmental and church authorities. These newcomers obtained work in various industries, railway yards, city construction projects, and small businesses of shoemaking, fruit and vegetable peddling, barbering and the needle trades. In politics they remained under represented and had to cope with the legacy of Al Capone and the substratum of the Sicilian underworld of the 1920s and the Prohibition decade. The second generation of Italians born after the First World War became middle-class Americans and overcame the poverty, crime, and political ignorance of their ethnic past. They were no longer "birds of passage," but settlers and Americans.

Another Mediterranean group, the Greeks, despite their great classical legacy, also came from a poor rural culture and turned Chicago into a success story for themselves. Although a humble rural folk, Chicago's Hellene immigrants were entrepreneurially talented and by 1920 some 10,000 were self-employed in small businesses ranging from pushcarts to restaurants, retail and wholesale houses, and some of Chicago's first ice cream parlors. Greeks were also one of the leading groups in keeping their homeland culture and language alive in Chicago by after-school and church-school language and culture programs.

The year 1930 began the Depression decade and thousands were beleaguered by unemployment. The worst times came in 1933 when firemen, policemen, teachers, and public employers faced "payless paydays." By then, the city's staggering debt for unpaid bills and salaries reached $133 million as public services declined. But thereafter, the federal government's Reconstruction Finance Corporation would help to put the city's finances back in order. The Works Progress Administration also helped to restore jobs for hundreds of Chicagoans and also set off several new public building projects. Many Chicagoans like Harold Washington, who later would become the city's first black mayor, found employment with the federal Civilian Conservation Corp working in CCC camps in Michigan.

Chicago's police department under Mayor Ed Kelly also began to work vigorously at crime control to reduce the city's reputation as a "haven for gangsters and criminals," a carry over from Prohibition-era's Al Capone and gangland organized crime. Capone was sent to prison in 1931. Prohibition ended in 1933 and thereafter crime rates began to decline over the next decade and a half—murder and robbery rates would drop 32% and 76% respectively by 1947.

After hitting a low point in 1933, the economy was helped somewhat by the 1933 Century of Progress world's fair that brought thousands of tourists to the city. By 1941, Chicago's economy was slowly recovering and this recovery would accelerate when the demands for war-time production and military training would soar in the city after the bombing of Pearl Harbor on December 7.

One

WARTIME CHICAGO

Unlike World War I when Chicago was a hotbed of anti-war and, at times, pro-German sentiment (due in large part to the city's enormous German-American population and the political manipulations of the city's mercurial mayor William Hale "Big Bill" Thompson), the Windy City was united in its World War II effort against the Axis powers. Besides signing up for military service, Chicagoans, men and women alike, rallied to the call for increased wartime domestic production.

Though not on the war's front lines—Chicagoans aided the war effort through the rationing of food and gasoline. Shortages, especially in meat and coffee—gave many local citizens a symbolic shared feeling of sacrifice with the servicemen overseas.

Seldom discussed is the energy and effort various Chicago neighborhoods put into the war effort. From fast growing victory gardens to mini-monuments to local servicemen—Chicago, the "City of Neighborhoods," saw all of its geographic parts vie for recognition and honor in a ethnic mosaic of patriotism.

Also during the war, Chicago became an important center for the American military effort with downtown hotels accommodating thousands of troops who were either in training or passing through Chicago to the Pacific or Atlantic fronts. Two side-wheeled paddle-lake steamers had their decks cleared and were converted into makeshift aircraft carriers (the USS *Wolverine* and USS *Sable*) for thousands of pilots who were training at the Glenview Naval Air Station. The two ships parked at Navy Pier and then sailed out in the daylight to receive pilots practicing their landings. Military servicemen were well treated in Chicago with city servicemen's centers, the Travelers Aid Society, and other civic groups providing USOs and travel lounges to accommodate them.

Servicemen were offered free cab and bus rides locally, travel information, and recreation halls such as the architecturally famous Auditorium Theater, which was handed over to the USO and became a military lounge and a bowling alley.

The nearby Great Lakes Naval Training Station provided training for nearly one third of the nation's naval recruits in World War II. Some nationally prominent figures also fit into Chicago's war effort. In January 1942, world heavyweight boxing champion Joe Louis volunteered for the U.S. Army in Chicago, just a few days before he was scheduled to report for the draft, and just two days after he had defeated a challenger and retained his prize fighting title.

In February 1942, Chicago military aviator Edward "Butch" O'Hare shot down five Japanese war planes threatening the American aircraft carrier *Lexington* and became a national hero. (O'Hare's success marked one of the few early American victories after the Japanese destruction of the American fleet at Pearl Harbor on December 7, 1941.) Called back to the U.S., O'Hare was awarded the Congressional Medal of Honor by President Franklin Roosevelt for his gallant performance. A year later in 1943, he was shot down in aerial combat and died. Later, in 1955, when airline passenger traffic began at Old Orchard Field, the airport facility was renamed O'Hare Field in Butch's honor.

Chicago's civilian population also engaged vigorously in manufacturing war materials. Hundreds of women, inspired by the popular "Rosie the Riveter" figure, worked in the defense industries replacing the male labor force, which had been inducted into the military. Several thousand black tenant farmers from the south also migrated to Chicago to help fill in the wartime labor shortages. Defense plants sprang up all over the Chicago metropolitan area with aircraft engines for example being manufactured in several area auto plants and other facilities, e.g. Douglas Aircraft turned out C-54 cargo planes at Orchard Field. Chicago colleges also played an important role for it was at the University of Chicago's Stagg Field where physicist Enrico Fermi and company brought about the first nuclear chain reaction and atomic fission. This scientific breakthrough would lead to the Manhattan Project and America's winning the race to develop the atomic bomb, the use of which brought World War II to an end in August 1945. After the war the peaceful use of atomic energy research was centered at the Argonne and later Fermi Laboratories.

The *Chicago Sun* War Atlas was a very informative supplement covering the Pacific and Atlantic wars with maps detailing the Pearl Harbor bombing, the location of ships sunk in the Atlantic by German submarines, Axis and Soviet battle lines in Russia, Japanese conquests in Southeast Asia, the General MacArthur defense line at Bataan in the Philippines, and the locations of U.S. and Japanese naval bases.

War Years

Chicago's Russian-Jewish Maxwell Street settlers as they began to move up the occupation and income scales in the late 1930s and 1940s migrated out to more attractive Chicago neighborhoods such as Lawndale where many of them moved their family businesses. (Courtesy of Rose Pollack.)

Benny Goodman came from the Maxwell Street Jewish settlement, studied music at Jane Addams' Hull House, became a saxophonist and band leader, and in 1940 was declared to be America's "King of Swing." (Courtesy of University of Illinois Chicago Urban Archives.)

Italian-American Devotees of Santa Maria, an old country village saint, paraded through neighborhood streets in the mid-1940s, keeping a cultural link to their Italian villages or their parent's birthplaces. (Courtesy of Dominic Candeloro's Italians in Chicago project.)

One of Chicago's best-known ethnic communities is "Chinatown," founded in 1910 with laundries, restaurants, and other businesses and remains to the present an ethnic core community. (Courtesy of Susan Moy.)

When Japan attacked China in the 1930s and began to occupy Chinese territory, Chicago's Chinese-Americans protested vigorously in Chicago's Chinatown. (Courtesy of Susan Moy.)

Some of Chicago's Chinese-Americans are pictured here buying war relief bonds to help the victims of Sino-Japanese war. (Courtesy of Susan Moy.)

The day after Pearl Harbor, two marines walk their post at the U.S. Naval Reserve armory on Randolph Street. (Courtesy of *Chicago Sun-Times*, December 1941.)

66TH YEAR—288. | **MONDAY, DECEMBER 8, 1941**— THIRTY-FOUR PAGES. | Telephone DEArborn 1111 ★ THREE CENTS

JAPANESE BOMB MANILA!
CONGRESS DECLARES WAR

★ ★ ★ ★ ★ ★

Guam, Wake, Islands Seized: Toky

'3 Yank Warships Sunk'; Tokyo Claims Sea Rule

'Nipponese Fleet Intact So Far'; 'Six U. S. Cruisers Damaged.'

Tokyo, Tuesday, Dec. 9.— (Official radio picked up by AP)—The Japanese asserted today that they had won naval supremacy over the United States in the Pacific, claiming by official or unofficial reports the destruction of two American battleships and an aircraft carrier and the damaging of four battleships and six cruisers.

These, declared the Japanese, were the principal results of the first shock of their air-naval offensive.

The claim to supremacy appeared in a commentary-resume broadcast by Domei, which said that any force

Huge Losses Admitted by White House

BY PAUL R. LEACH.
Special Dispatch from a Staff Correspondent.
Washington, Dec. 8.— Japan's surprise attack upon Pearl Harbor and the island of Oahu resulted in 3,000 casualties, half of them fatal, the destruction of one battleship and one destroyer, damage to several other ships and Army airfields.

That announcement was made by White House secretary, Stephen Early, as President Roosevelt prepared his war declaration message for personal delivery to a joint session of Congress.

Early Reads Statement.

The following statement, written in longhand upon a piece of gold embossed White House stationery, was read by Mr. Early

Radio Reporter Relates Firing of Air Field in Philippines.

New York, Dec. 8.—(P)—The Tokyo radio tonight reported under a Shanghai dateline that both Guam and Wake islands were under the Japanese flag. The broadcast was heard here by CBS.

BULLETIN.
New York, Dec. 8.—(P)—An NBC reporter, broadcasting in the midst of a Jap air attack early Tuesday morning on Manila, said there had been "terrific damage," including the apparent destruction of the gasoline supply at Nichols Air Field.

There was a lull in the action some time after 3 a. m. (Tuesday) Manila time, but at 3:41 a. m., the anti-aircraft fire reopened, said the radio reporter, Don Bell. He add-

PACIFIC COAST ON THE ALERT; GUARD PLANTS

San Francisco, Dec. 8.—(UP)—The Pacific coast, from Alaska to

A United Nation

Today, the United States is at war. We write these words in sorrow. We write them also with a sense, undoubtedly shared by a vast number of Americans, not exactly of relief at this tragic ending of the long nerve strain to which we have been subjected, but of deep faith that all is somehow for the best.

We have tried in every reasonable way to avoid what has happened. At the hands both of Hitler and Japan, we have been patient and long-suffering. To everyone, the truth should at last be apparent, as The Daily News has for months been explaining, that Hitler's plans, in conjunction with Japan's, included,—at his own chosen moment, under the Tokyo-Berlin-Rome alliance—a blitz attack on the United States. Sooner or later, it had to come.

Thanks now to Japan, the deep division of opinion that has rent and partly paralyzed our country will be swiftly healed. It cannot be otherwise. Once more, we shall be a united people, firm in a single determination—to maintain our liberties by the complete and utter defeat of our foes.

Unite in War On Axis, China Urges Allies

BY LELAND STOWE.
SPECIAL RADIO.
To The Chicago Daily News Foreign Service.
Copyright 1941, The Chicago Daily News, Inc.
Chungking, Dec. 8.—China has

BRITAIN JOINS U. S. IN WAR ON JAPANESE

Churchill Keeps Pledge to America; Assails Tokyo's Treachery.

London, Dec. 8—(AP)— Britain, like the United States, declared war today on the Tokyo government, without waiting for Washington first to formulate an American declaration.

"Said Prime Minister Churchill):

"It only remains now for the two great democracies to face their tasks with whatever strength God may give them."

At the same time Britain made allies of Thailand and Free China.

Prime Minister Churchill told the House of Commons that instruc-

Congress Acts On F.D.R. Pl

Senate Votes 82 to 0, House 388 on War Resolution; Roosevelt Hits 'Shocking Aggression.'

[The text of President Roosevelt's message to Congress asking a declaration of war on Japan is on page 3.]

BY PAUL R. LEACH.
Special Dispatch from a Staff Correspondent.
Washington, Dec. 8—The United States has declared formal war against the Japanese Empire, to avenge the unprovoked attack upon its territory since 1812, with only one dissenting vote in the Congress.

Within 33 minutes after President Roosevelt had delivered a short, dramatic message to a joint session in the House chamber, where he was cheered time and again, House and Senate had voted upon a state of war resolution.

The Senate voted unanimously, 82 to 0.

The House vote was 388 to 1. The one dissenting vote was cast by a woman, Representative Jeanette Rankin of Missoula, Mont. She had voted against war with Germany in 1917. Amid hisses and boos from the floor and

The day after Pearl Harbor the city's afternoon newspaper, the *Chicago Daily News*, headlines the bombing of Manila and more importantly that Congress had declared war on Japan. Notice the insert "A United Nation." *Daily News* editors do not mention Germany, but rather use its leader's name, Hitler, as if he were a country. (Courtesy of *Chicago Sun-Times*, December 1941.)

18

This is a remarkable photo of the *Abendpost*—an American newspaper printed in German. This front page is dated December 8, 1941 and it declares the United States is at war. However, notice the two paragraph English language insert under the heading "We are at war." Here, the *Abendpost* editors tell one and all that German Americans will support their country against Japan. A few days later Germany declared war on the United States. We do not know if another English insert appeared in the newspaper. (Courtesy of University of Illinois Urban Collection.)

Taylor Street resident Tony Grippo, holding newspaper, is seen with a couple of neighbors reading about Germany and Italy's declaration of war against the United States a few days after Pearl Harbor. (Courtesy of *Chicago Sun-Times*, December 1941.)

Less than one week after Pearl Harbor, Morris Weiss, a Maxwell Street dry goods store owner, proudly throws out all of his Japanese-made merchandise. (Courtesy of *Chicago Sun-Times*, December 1941.)

Recruitment and Training

More than a year before the United States entered World War II army posts like Fort Sheridan began to get busy. This photo shows Chicagoan James Manning filling out his official enlistment papers. Notice all the typewriters are in a neat row. (Courtesy of *Chicago Sun-Times*, November 1940.)

This is another pre-war snapshot taken at Fort Sheridan. The men walking between the ranks of soldiers are 46 new recruits from Cook County. (Courtesy of *Chicago Sun-Times*, May 1941.)

This June 1942 photo of Chicago metro area military inductees includes a large number of Italian Americans from suburban Chicago Heights. (Courtesy of Dominic Candeloro's *Italians in Chicago* project.)

Here, Navy Shore Patrolmen line up for a morning march at Chicago's Grant Park. With the Great Lakes Naval training station nearby, Chicago was the big city home for thousands of servicemen. (Courtesy of City of Chicago Civil Defense Commission.)

During World War II, Chicago became a major training site for the military. Two Chicago hotels, the Hilton and the Congress, became barracks for several thousand troops. The city's Navy Pier became a training site for sailors. (Courtesy of UIC Historians Office.)

Two Lake Michigan steamers—USS *Sable* and USS *Wolverine*—were converted into aircraft carriers for training navy pilots. Glenview Naval Airmen flew to the two converted steamers to learn how to land on aircraft carriers, which were the key landing fields in the Pacific Ocean war theater. (Courtesy of Glenview Naval Air Station Collection.)

Ration Impact

This August 1942 photo shows State and Madison, one of Chicago's busiest corners. The war effort slowed but did not halt summertime street reconstruction projects. (Courtesy of City of Chicago "Report to the People.")

This is a view of Michigan Avenue from the Stevens (Hilton) hotel looking south. This picture was taken at 9:00 a.m. on a weekday. Wartime gas rationing drastically reduced car traffic in the city even during rush hour. (Courtesy of *Chicago Sun-Times*, December 1942.)

November 1942. Three Michigan Avenue businessmen are seen making sales calls in the West Randolph Street market neighborhood. This new type of "horsepower" was not for everyone, but all Chicagoans were deeply impacted by the wartime gas-rationing program. (Courtesy of *Chicago Sun-Times*, November 1942.)

North State Street is pictured here during a regular weekday/workday. Traffic is barely visible, as the wartime gas-rationing policy remained a major hindrance to private automotive traffic. (Courtesy of *Chicago Sun-Times*, February 1945.)

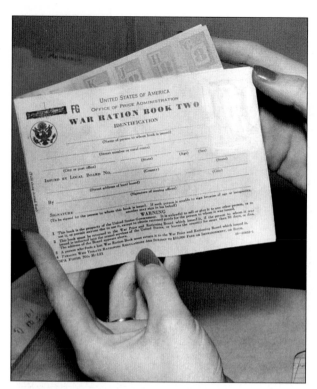

Shown here is a ration book identification card. The Office of Price Administration (OPA) managed this critical wartime activity that impacted every American family. (Courtesy of *Chicago Sun-Times*, January 1943.)

Wartime food rationing was sometimes a confusing undertaking. Citizens were given coupon books that created a "point rationing" system for most food items. This photo shows a government official explaining the process at a North Michigan Avenue grocery store. (Courtesy of *Chicago Sun-Times*, June 1943.)

December 1942. The White City Meat market at 73rd and Vincennes closed its doors due to the wartime meat shortage. One year into the war people like Mrs. Harry Wirtz and her daughter Madeline (shown in photo) faced the daunting prospect of finding butcher shops still in business. (Courtesy of *Chicago Sun-Times*, December 1942.)

George Gerules, a Bridgeport neighborhood butcher, takes a snooze at his shop at 3527 S. Halsted. Limited meat supply coupled with limited ration books gave Mr. Gerules plenty of workweek relaxation periods known at the time as "frozen meat days." (Courtesy of *Chicago Sun-Times*, March 1943.)

A classic photo—coffee day at the Jewel food store located at Wilson and Racine Avenues on the city's Northeast Side. Individuals lucky enough to have coffee coupons are shown waiting in a long line hoping that the store's supply lasts long enough for them to purchase this scarce commodity. Notice no one is waiting to enter Jewel's next-door rival Kroger. Obviously no coffee day there! (Courtesy of *Chicago Sun-Times*, November 1942.)

Children and adults collected old tires, paper, metal scrap, and tin for recycling into war material by defense manufacturers. (Courtesy of Civil Defense Collection.)

Rationing and shortages made many Chicagoans plant their own crops in their neighborhood. These enterprises were called Victory Gardens. This photo shows a group of woman at 82nd and Jeffery Streets cleaning an old scrap heap and readying it for planting. (Courtesy of *Chicago Sun-Times*, April 1943.)

In April 1943 Charles Vavrosky (kneeling) is helped out by his Whitney School classmates in starting a Victory Garden in his Southwest Side neighborhood. (Courtesy of *Chicago Sun-Times*, April 1943.)

Patriotism

During World War II, most Chicago neighborhoods found different ways to support the war effort. One such activity was to square off a piece of land, usually on a street corner, insert a flagpole and display the flag everyday. This photo depicts a flag dedication ceremony at the corner of Racine and Van Buren streets in a predominantly Italian West Side neighborhood. (Courtesy of *Chicago Sun-Times*, October 1942.)

Another flag dedication—this photo was taken on the city's South Side at the corner of Cottage Grove and 72nd Streets. Part of the purpose of the flag dedication activity was to honor neighborhood service men and women involved in the war effort. (Courtesy of *Chicago Sun-Times*, October 1942.)

Many Nisei, or second-generation, Japanese Americans, despite the pain of being put into relocation centers, volunteered to serve in the U.S. military forces during World War II. Above is a picture of a Nisei soldier who served in the Italian campaign. (Courtesy of Mosako Osako.)

Two proud but emotionally weary Japanese-born American mothers display flags signifying that each has four sons serving in the American armed forces during World War II. (Courtesy of War Relocation Authority.)

"But we didn't mean CHICAGO typewriters, sir!"

This cartoon appeared in *Victory Magazine*. It plays upon the notion that in Chicago gangsters often called submachine guns "typewriters." The cartoon outraged Chicago Mayor Edward J. Kelly who sent a letter of protest to the U.S. Army's information chief, Elmer Davis. (Courtesy of *Chicago Sun-Times*, August 1942.)

Women

Women defense workers at International Harvester are seen here assembling torpedoes for American military aircraft. Women played a key role in helping to fulfill the manufacturing manpower shortages caused by war. (Courtesy of City of Chicago.)

Women defense workers entered into wartime occupations that had previously been dominated by all male workers, thus leading to the new wartime title of "Rosie the Riveter." (Courtesy of *Chicago Sun-Times*, January 1943.)

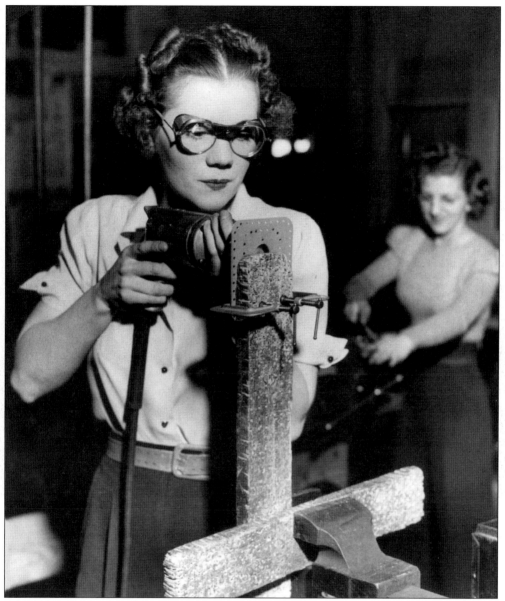

February 1943. Miss Louise Stellon, a South Side Chicagoan, is shown training for a job at Pullman Standard Car Manufacturing Company. This factory became a huge cargo plane plant as part of a government plan to boost aircraft expansion. Half the new workers recruited were women, thereby avoiding serious wartime employee shortages. (Courtesy of *Chicago Sun-Times*, February 1943.)

Women ordinance workers are seen repairing two vehicles at a near South Side military garage. (Courtesy of *Chicago Sun-Times*, June 1944.)

A Palmer House reception was held for the women employees of Philco Radio. Both the US Army and Navy presented the workers the coveted "E" (effort) award for improved production. (Courtesy of *Chicago Sun-Times*, November 1942.)

The Barber–Greene Company of Aurora, Illinois is seen receiving its "E" (effort) award for increasing production during wartime. (Courtesy of *Chicago Sun-Times*, August 1942.)

This November 1943 scene shows State and Madison in downtown Chicago. A soldier is urging Chicagoans to sign up for war related work. (Courtesy of Civil Defense File, Kennedy Collection.)

The Women's Army Corp, known as WACS, helped to solve the military manpower shortages in World War II. Seen here a volunteer WAC worker at Chicago's Union railroad station. (Courtesy of U.S. National Archives.)

Hospitality and Service

The Chicago Commission on National Defense opened one of the nation's first Servicemen's Centers in 1941, which was located on Washington Street, one block from city hall. (Courtesy of City of Chicago.)

Mayor Kelly reviews troops that participated in ceremonies on the occasion of awards to himself and Mrs. Kelly by the War Department and American Veterans Committee of the Roosevelt College Chapter for their leadership of Chicago Servicemen's Centers. (Courtesy of City of Chicago.)

The mayor's wife, Mrs. Edward Kelly, plays the piano for a group of soldiers at the Chicago Servicemen's Center in 1944. (Courtesy of City of Chicago.)

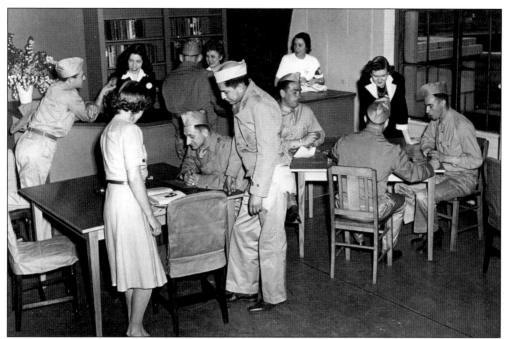

U.S. Troops at the Travelers Aid Society Transit Lounge receiving travel information on their transit from Chicago to other military encampments. (Courtesy of University of Illinois, Chicago Urban Archives.)

The Travelers Aid Society, founded by Hull House residents, became affiliated with the U.S.O. during World War II and provided aid, information, and transit lounge programs for 500,000 traveling U.S. Servicemen. (Courtesy of University of Illinois, Chicago Urban Archives.)

German-born music director Frederick Stock became conductor of the Chicago Symphony Orchestra in 1905, when the founding father, Theodore Thomas passed away. Stock was ranked as one of the leading classical music conductors in the nation and continued to direct the Chicago Symphony until his death on October 28, 1942. (Courtesy of Chicago Symphony Orchestra.)

Chicago's famous Auditorium building (center right), built in the late-19th century and designed by Louis Sullivan & Dankmar Adler had its huge theater's stage turned into a servicemen's bowling alley during World War II. (Courtesy of Roosevelt University.)

Here, on Christmas Day at the Auditorium building, two Chicagoans, Frank Elkenborg (Santa) and Ruth Baskin, help a private from Kansas select a Christmas present for himself. Rumor had it that he took a long time making up his mind. (Courtesy of *Chicago Sun-Times*, December 1942.)

This 1943 Chicago Christmas-time photo depicts volunteer women workers wrapping gifts for military personnel in Chicago. Sponsored by the *Times* newspaper, this huge effort was headquartered at the Auditorium Service Men's Center in the famous Auditorium building. (Courtesy of *Chicago Sun-Times*, December 1943.)

On behalf of the Service men, I am expressing appreciation for the installation & maintenance of the 12 alleys from the Bowling Proprietors Assn. of Greater Chicago.

Mrs. Edward J. Kelly

Mayor Edward J. Kelly and his wife are pictured at the ribbon cutting ceremony that opened the twelve bowling alleys on the Auditorium Theater stage in 1942. (Courtesy of Roosevelt University.)

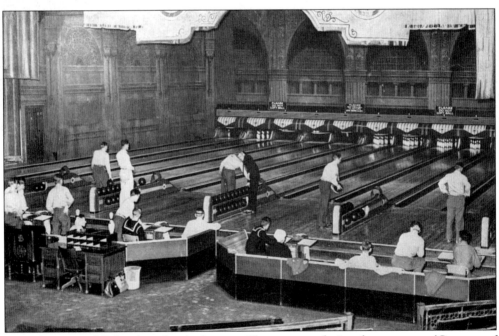

Here, American GI's bowl on the Auditorium Theater stage during the war years. (Courtesy of Roosevelt University.)

Wartime Celebs

President Franklin Roosevelt awards a medal to Chicago's American air ace, Edward "Butch" O'Hare who shot down five Japanese airplanes that had targeted the U.S. carrier *Lexington*. Butch later lost his life in aerial combat in 1943, but one of the nation's busiest airports would be named after him when Orchard Field became O'Hare Field. (Courtesy of City of Chicago: Graphics and Reproduction Center.)

In 1942, Italian-born physicist Enrico Fermi produced the first nuclear reaction in a secret room underneath the University of Chicago's Stagg field stadium. This splitting of the atom led to the Manhattan project and to America's triumph as the first nation to develop the atomic bomb and nuclear power. (Courtesy of NARA's Federal Regional Great Lakes Archives Center, Chicago.)

From left to right, Aaron Payne, a Chicago official, greets Mrs. Marva Louis and her husband, boxing world-champion Joe Louis, in his army uniform. (Courtesy of Urban Historical Collection.)

Montgomery Ward's board chairman, Sewell Avery, refused to comply with the federal War Labor Board's orders to end a strike. In April 1944, the federal government seized control of Wards and on April 27, U.S. Attorney General Francis Biddle ordered chairman Avery evicted from Ward's headquarters. (Courtesy of *Chicago Daily News*.)

The federal government took over control of Montgomery Wards Chicago and Illinois offices and plants in 1944 after a company conflict with the War Labor Board. Above, on April 27, 1944, U.S. troops stand guard outside of the company's Chicago office. (Courtesy of Montgomery Wards & Co.)

War Ends

West Side Chicagoan, Pvt. Walter Platt, celebrates V-E Day with two lovely South Side co-eds. Private Platt is proudly wearing his European purple heart. (Courtesy of *Chicago Sun-Times*, May 1945.)

Factory workers at Chicago Gaylord Products Inc. take a short break to cheer the victory in Europe. As seen in the photo this celebration was somewhat muted due to the continuing war against Japan in the Pacific. (Courtesy of *Chicago Sun-Times*, May 1945.)

South Side soldier Nicholas Boersma catches a nap at the Chicago Service Men's Center at 176 W. Washington after reading that the war in Europe was over. (Courtesy of *Chicago Sun-Times*, May 1945.)

A crowd gathers around a car radio at the corner of State and Madison to hear the latest news about the dropping of the atomic bomb on the Japanese city of Nagasaki. (Courtesy of *Chicago Sun-Times*, August 1945.)

This headline from the *Chicago Times* declared that peace was due to the Japanese surrender. Also in the headline is the hope that gas rationing was also over. (Courtesy of *Chicago Sun-Times*, August 1945.)

Three North Side youngsters—Linda Tellesfin, Donald and Robert Weissman—are curbside at State and Randolph watching the V-J celebration in downtown Chicago. The city's response to V-J day was far more rambunctious then the V-E day happenings in May. (Courtesy of *Chicago Sun-Times*, August 1945.)

Here we have a requisite victory photo of a paratrooper kissing a young Chicago woman war worker during a spontaneous Loop V-J celebration. (Courtesy of *Chicago Sun-Times*, August 1945.)

Italian prisoners of war working at Vaughan General Hospital cheer the news of the Japanese surrender. (Courtesy of *Chicago Sun-Times*, August 1945.)

Two

POST-WAR CHICAGO

The coming of peace in 1945 brought serious concerns to Chicago's political leaders and some citizens who feared that the pre-war Depression decade of joblessness, want, and poverty might be returning. It also stirred up concern about a possible repeat of post World War I's race riots, red scares, and anarchist bombings. But post-WW II Chicago experienced prosperity, peaceful times, and a population boom. Chicago's population soared from 3,300,000 million in 1940 to 3,620,000 by 1950, the high point of the city's population in the 20th century.

Post-war Chicago experienced a surge of economic and industrial growth. The pent-up demand created by wartime rationing, wartime savings with War Bond buying, and returning servicemen created an enormous demand for consumer products including meat (which no longer was rationed), automobiles, hundreds of consumer products, and new housing made possible by federal subsidies and low interest rates. Thousands of veterans entered college and technical school training, which also meant that the fear of a surplus labor force and unemployment were also overcome.

One military veteran who enrolled in the fall of 1947 at Roosevelt College under the GI Bill was named Harold Washington; he would later become Chicago's first black mayor.

Slum clearance and new public housing projects were implemented to improve living conditions for many low-income Chicagoans. At the same time suburbanization, spurred on by new highways and government backed low mortgages, expanded Chicago from a city to a region. Chicago was alive and changes were happening to all aspects of its citizens' lifestyles—from where they lived to where they worked and played.

Adding to the post World War II demographic shifting was the massive influx of African-Americans from the south. Though race was certainly a city issue prior to World War II—after the war and for most of the rest of the century—race became the issue in Chicago politics and socio-economics.

Lastly, and perhaps most astounding in the post-war era—in 1945 the Chicago Cubs won the National League pennant and played the Detroit Tigers in the World Series (they lost). According to Sam Greenberg, a disabled veteran who saw all the series games at Wrigley Field, "I am now close to ninety years of age—I plan on living long enough to see another World Series game at Wrigley Field . . . no matter how long it takes." Clearly, post-World War II optimism and hope still smolders in the hearts of Chicago's "greatest generation."

Chicago's well known "blood and guts" local politics took a breather during World War II. Incumbent Mayor Edward J. Kelly (appointed in 1933 to replace the assassinated Anton Cermak) was a busy wartime mayor about town. However, charges of rampant corruption and political incompetence made his post-war rule last less than two years.

In what amounted to an internal party coup—the Cook County Democratic Central Committee, led by returning veteran Col. Jacob Arvey, dumped Mayor Kelly for businessman Martin Kennelly before the 1947 mayoral campaign. Though our photos show that all involved smiled a lot—even at each other—behind the scenes former Mayor Kelly was outraged at his ousting.

Ironically, eight years later Martin Kennelly himself was victim to another mayoral coup when the new local Democratic Party chairman, Richard J. Daley, denied the incumbent party support for the 1955 Democratic mayoral primary. Oh yes—the 1955 endorsed mayoral candidate was Chairman Daley, who bested Kennelly in a heated and hard fought mayoral primary.

At the state and national level Chicago politics raced to prominence following the war. In the now near legendary 1948 Presidential contest the underdog incumbent candidate Harry S. Truman used the city as a focal point for his Midwest campaign. Aiding Mr. Truman in Illinois was an early version of a "dream ticket" as the Democrats nominated University of Chicago professor and former alderman Paul Douglas for U.S. Senate and well-known political figure Adlai Stevenson for Illinois governor. Ironically, both of these political giants were viewed early in the campaign as throw away candidates in an expected big Republican year—instead, each won in a landslide and helped give Mr. Truman Illinois' electoral votes.

Four years later, Gov. Adlai Stevenson would win the Democratic presidential nomination at the party's national convention in Chicago. Unfortunately for Stevenson, his Republican presidential foe was former general and war hero Dwight D. Eisenhower, who crushed Stevenson nationally and even carried the Governor's home state of Illinois.

The photos in the book try to recapture the spirit and pain of the war years and the exuberance and challenges of the post-war era. Chicago would lose its most famous pre-war description of being "hog butcher to the world" (the famous stockyards would diminish and eventually disappear as a huge city employer). Instead, it would become once again the recognized transportation hub of the nation and according to most of its citizens, assume the title "the city that works." Strong political leadership coupled with a renewed "I will" vigor would see the city soar in the late 1940s and 1950s as many Chicagoans saw their standard of living rise to match their dreams. This upward mobility did not reach everyone, and in the 1960s Chicago and much of the rest of the country would experience the tragedy of urban riots and cries for equality and fairness in all aspects of American life.

Culture

(*right*) Following the war, many Chicago communities established "Honor Roll" plaques for their neighborhood veterans. This impressive structure stood at the corner of Sheridan and Eastwood Avenues on the city's Northeast Side. (Courtesy of *Chicago Sun-Times*, December 1945.)

(*left*) Chicago's Navy Pier, which had served as a military training base in World War II, was leased by the University of Illinois in 1946 and converted into a college to accommodate veterans seeking higher education under the GI Bill. (Courtesy of UIC Historian's Office.)

(*right*) American veterans lined up in the University of Illinois Navy Pier bookstore in 1946 to buy books for their college classes, paid for by the G.I. Bill. (Courtesy of UIC Historian's Office.)

On May 28, 1949, the new North State Street bridge over the Chicago River was renamed the Bataan–Corregidor Memorial Bridge. In attendance at the dedication was General Douglas MacArthur. This photo shows the bridge a few months prior to its completion. (Courtesy of City of Chicago: Graphics and Reproduction Center.)

Chicago in 1949 opened the Bataan–Corregidor Memorial Bridge to honor Maywood and the Illinois National Guardsmen and American servicemen who had been captured by the Japanese invaders in the Philippines in April of 1942 and were forced to march 65 miles to a prison camp. The "death march" was deadly; dozens of prisoners were clubbed, beaten, bayoneted, and run over and crushed by Japanese war machines. (Courtesy of Kennelly Collection.)

Pictured at the opening of the new Universal International Film Exchange in Chicago on February 9, 1948 are, from left to right, F.T. Murray, Hostess Dee Balla, and Irv Kupeinet. (Courtesy of Urban Historical Collection.)

A welcoming tea was held at the downtown YWCA (59 East Monroe) for war brides from Europe. Most of these women are English and all met their servicemen husbands in their native countries. (Courtesy of Chicago Sun-Times, October 1946.)

After World War II, downtown Chicago once again became a night-spot Mecca for city residents. One of the towns' most famous Loop restaurants was Fritzel's located at State and Lake. Always busy, parking became a huge problem especially on weekend nights and anytime during the Christmas holiday season. This photo was taken in December of 1952.

Here they are, the National League champs the Chicago Cubs in October 1945, prior to the World Series against the Detroit Tigers. As almost everyone in Chicagoland knows, the Cubs lost the series and have not been back to the "autumn classic" since 1945. (Courtesy of *Chicago Sun-Times*, October 1945.).

Post-war Chicago factories refocus their energies on consumer products. This photo from October 1945 shows new electric stoves replacing tanks on the assembly line. (Courtesy of *Chicago Sun-Times*, October 1945.)

South-Sider Betty Metzger is shown here in April 1947 demonstrating an old-style washing machine. After World War II, the government launched a massive war surplus sale to dispose of out of date appliances—like manual washing machines. (Courtesy of *Chicago Sun-Times*, April 1947.)

New automatic washer/dryers became available to the consumer-starved post-war American public. These smooth countertop side-by-side appliances were a huge upgrade from the old pre-war manual washers. This photo was taken in March of 1955. (Courtesy of *Chicago Sun-Times*, March 1955.)

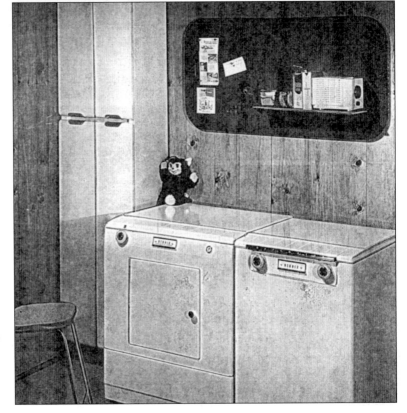

Ethnic Celebrations

Some 30,000 Japanese Americans who had been moved off of the West Coast by President Franklin Roosevelt in 1942 moved to Chicago where most remained and formed the core of an ethnic community. Pictured above is an image of American-born or second-generation (known as Nisei) with their festival queen being introduced to Mayor Kennelly. (Courtesy of Kennelly Collection.)

Mary Ann Akiyama presenting Japanese-American Year Book to Mayor Kennelly. April 7, 1948.

A Japanese-American child, Mary Ann Akiyama, presents the Japanese-Americans Yearbook on April 7, 1948 to Mayor Kennelly. (Courtesy of Kennelly Collection.)

President Truman's visit to Chicago
Swedish Pioneer Centennial
Friday June 4, 1948

President Truman

Mayor Kennelly

President Truman visited Chicago on June 4, 1948 during the Swedish Pioneer Centennial, celebrating Swedish immigration to Chicago. (Courtesy of Kennelly Collection.)

The celebration of Ireland's Independence Day was held on April 18, 1949 at Chicago's Palmer House Grand Ballroom. Seated from left to right are Chicago Mayor Kennelly and, next to him, Sean MacBride, Minister of External Affairs Ireland. Standing are two more Illinois politicians of Irish ancestry, State's Attorney John Boyle and Judge Michael Igoe. (Courtesy of Kennelly Collection.)

President Harry Truman (left) and Mayor Martin Kennelly (middle) meet Sweden's Prince Bertil (right) visiting Chicago to celebrate the Swedish-American Pioneer Centennial on June 4, 1948. (Courtesy of Kennelly Collection.)

Prince Bertil of Sweden visits Chicago to celebrate the Swedish Pioneer Centennial, June 3, 1948 and is given a plaque by Mayor Martin Kennelly. Chicago's Swedish Americans were becoming conscious of maintaining a cultural tie to the old country and among the many things done was the establishment a few years later of the Swedish American Historical Quarterly. (Courtesy of Kennelly Collection.)

Mayor Kennelly greeted a visiting Paris opera ballet company on September 14, 1948. This kind of interest in music would later lead, in 1954, to the founding of the Lyric Opera Company in Chicago. (Courtesy of Kennelly Collection.)

The German Day Associations Annual Celebration is greeted and welcomed on June 26, 1949 by a group of American political leaders including Chicago's mayor, U.S. Attorney General Thomas Clark, U.S. Senator William Langer, and State Legislator Charlie Weber. (Courtesy of Kennelly Collection.)

Attending Rededication Week of Labor Management Day on July 1, 1948, Chicago Mayor Kennelly recognized the various immigrant and ethnic groups that had provided workers for the Hawthorne Corporation. (Courtesy of Kennelly Collection.)

Mayor Kennelly greets vocalist and opera singer Lauritz Melchoir at a music festival held at Chicago's Palmer House Hotel on August 19, 1949. Chicago mayors have long been supporters of music culture dating back to the 1891 founding of the Chicago Symphony Orchestra. (Courtesy of Kennelly Collection.)

Transportation: Rail

Chicago's first passenger subway opened in 1943 underneath State Street and was called a "masterpiece of engineering" by the city. Passenger usage went into high gear following the war. (Courtesy of City of Chicago's "Report to the People.")

On February 24, 1951, Mayor Kennelly opened up the Milwaukee-Dearborn-Congress subway system. This was an addition to the subways constructed a decade earlier and helped to relieve some of the downtown traffic congestion. (Courtesy of Kennelly Collection.)

President Harry Truman (center) is being greeted by Chicagoans Mike Berry (left) and then-State Legislator and Cook County Sheriff candidate Richard J. Daley in this rare photo taken at Midway Airfield in 1946 when passenger planes were still propeller driven. (Courtesy of City of Chicago: Graphics and Reproduction Center.)

This is a very early photo of O'Hare Field. It would eventually become the nation's busiest airport—a fact highlighted at its official dedication in 1963 when President John F. Kennedy said, "There is no airport in the world which serves so many people and so many airplanes. This is an extraordinary airport (and) an extraordinary city. . . ." (Courtesy of City of Chicago: Graphics and Reproduction Center.)

Edward "Butch" O'Hare was an "Ace" fighter pilot during World War II. In 1949 Chicago's Orchard Field was renamed O'Hare Airport in his honor. (Courtesy of City of Chicago: Graphics and Reproduction Center.)

This photo of "Butch" O'Hare in his fighter aircraft was taken after another successful dogfight. Also depicted on the plane are decals representing each Japanese plane shot down by O'Hare. (Courtesy of City of Chicago: Graphics and Reproduction Center.)

This is a photo of an official portrait of Edward "Butch" O'Hare. Chicago's local war hero did not survive the war—he was killed in combat—a fact that helped push the effort to rename Orchard Field in 1949. Ironically, the 1949 O'Hare Airport dedication took place a decade after Lt. O'Hare's father, Eddie O'Hare, an Al Capone-era hoodlum, was assassinated in a gangland hit while driving his car on the city's West Side. (Courtesy of City of Chicago: Graphics and Reproduction Center.)

Following World War II, air travel boomed in the United States and especially in Chicago. This photo shows Chicago's Midway Airport located on the city's Southwest Side. Originally called Municipal airport (dedicated in 1927), it was renamed Midway in 1949 to commemorate the victory at Midway Island during the war. For nearly two decades (1932-1950) it was known as the country's busiest airport but lack of space and the jet age ended its number one reign. (Courtesy of City of Chicago: Graphics and Reproduction Center.)

Midway Airport's brand new terminal opened in 1945. This state of the art facility allowed Midway (then called Municipal Airport) to handle for a while the surge in air traffic. (Courtesy of City of Chicago: Graphics and Reproduction Center.)

Inauguration of Helicopter Air Mail Service
Saturday August 20, 1949

Mayor Martin H. Kennelly

John Haderlein,
Acting Postmaster

As air mailing picked up in the post-war years, Chicago inaugurated Helicopter Air Mail Service on August 20, 1949. Pictured, from left to right, are Chicago Mayor Kennelly and Postmaster John Haderlein pushing a cart of mail bags to begin the service. The third man is unidentified. (Courtesy of Kennelly Collection Society Photo Service.)

Mayor Martin Kennelly greets Merrill Meigs at the opening of Northerly Island Airport on the Chicago lakefront in 1948. The airport's name would later be changed to Meigs Field in honor of the Chicago businessman and longtime airport advocate. In more recent times, Mayor Richard M. Daley worked to close Meigs Field and turn it into a public park. (Courtesy of Kennelly Collection.)

Meigs Field was dedicated on June 30, 1950. (Courtesy of Kennelly Collection.)

Transportation: Land

After World War II, Chicago experienced a five-fold increase in the number of motor vehicles passing through the metro area as it became one of the nation's leading trucking centers, which moved a quarter of the city's freight tonnage. Such increases necessitated additional highway and expressway construction. (Courtesy of Kennelly Collection.)

American automobile production went into high gear following the war. The car hungry public demanded big and bold autos to reflect their desire for freedom of movement and comfort. Shown here is the 1946 Cadillac—a car that embodied the new American spirit. (Courtesy of *Chicago Sun-Times*, September 1946.)

As Chicago's population grew rapidly in the post-war era with returning veterans, war workers, and Southern migrants, the traffic volume also soared. The city's population would crest in 1950 with 3.6 million. The improving economy also meant that thousands of families that could not afford automobiles in the prewar period could now buy cars. The increased traffic volume also forced the city to expand many roadways from two to four lane traffic. (Courtesy of Chicago "Report to the People.")

Post-war Chicago had a building boom of new super highways, bridges and underpasses, and four-lane roads to accommodate the increased traffic volume of freight trucks, cars, and buses. (Courtesy of Chicago "Report to the People.")

Post-war Chicagoans totally embraced the automobile age. Mayors Ed Kelly and Martin Kennelly tried to provide street and highway improvements in the city. However, it was not until 1955 when Richard J. Daley became mayor that the city's entire infrastructure modernization went into overdrive. Shown here is an early post-war road improvement for Damen Avenue on the city's far Southwest Side. (Courtesy of City of Chicago: Graphics and Reproduction Center.)

As motor vehicle sales increased to veterans and civilians in the post-war years, so did traffic congestion. The city responded by increasing its traffic control equipment with new high speed motorcycles. (Courtesy of Kennelly Collection.)

Chicago as a port city, which included docks at Lake Calumet, became a major shipping center receiving grains, iron ore, and coal for manufacturing—and for shipping out manufactured products. The completion of the Saint Lawrence Seaway enabled shipping to Europe, Africa, and even parts of Asia. (Courtesy of Chicago Assn. of Commerce/Industry.)

Slum Clearance

Slum clearance became a huge issue in Chicago following World War II. Out of date old buildings and massive new African-American migration from the south combined to produce a housing crisis in Chicago. This photo depicts the corner of Cottage Grove and 27th Streets on the city's near Southeast Side. Dilapidated housing in the foreground was eventually replaced by newer buildings, like the Prairie Shores 14-story relocation housing in the background. (Courtesy of City of Chicago: Graphics and Reproduction Center.)

The Chicago Land Clearance Commission was designated to study and clear deteriorated buildings. This photo of a South Side structure in the early 1950s shows vividly the depths of the city's housing crises. (Courtesy of City of Chicago: Graphics and Reproduction Center.)

Slum clearance is seen here taking place northwest of Chicago's Loop in the early 1950s. Enormous pressure was placed on the city to find replacement housing, since Chicago's population was peaking. (Courtesy of City of Chicago: Graphics and Reproduction Center.)

Policy: New Housing and Neighborhood Maintenance

Mayor Kennelly digs first spadeful of earth at groundbreak[ing]
ceremonies for Dearborn Homes. December 2, 1948

d. Robert E. Merriam

Robert R. Taylor, Chairman
Chicago Housing Authority

U.S. Congressman
James V. Buckley

Mayor Kennelly

U.S. Senator
Paul H. Douglas

Henry
Command[er]
of Illinois

Construction of the Dearborn Homes public housing project began on December 2, 1948 as Mayor Kennelly dug the first spade full of earth in the groundbreaking ceremony. Some 800 units of low-cost public housing would become available for black families that had migrated from the south. Pictured from left to right are Alderman Robert Merriam, a 1955 mayoral candidate; Robert Taylor, chair of the Chicago Housing Authority, after whom the city's largest public housing project was later named; Mayor Kennelly; and U.S. Senator Paul Douglas. From 1950 to 1959, the Chicago Housing Authority built additional Cabrini Green public housing buildings and by then the racial composition was 75 percent black. The 15-story high-rise tenements were great improvements over the slum housing they replaced. But after the 1980s, the decline of two-parent households characterized Cabrini and a decade and a half later, single-mothers, some only in their teens, made up 75 percent of the households. The lack of two-parent discipline saw crime rates soar and prompted the CHA to start deconstructing public high-rise tenements.(Courtesy of Kennelly Collection.)

On November 25, 1949, State Director of Revenue Richard J. Daley (left center) handed Mayor Martin Kennelly a deed to a vacant lot. The property was a gift from the members of the Richard J. Daley Youth Organization in Daley's Bridgeport neighborhood and was given in order that it be turned into a public playground. (Courtesy of Kennelly Collection.)

Race, politics, and economics made the building of new affordable housing after World War II a highly complicated and controversial issue. In most cases, the answer was high-rise public housing which at the time seemed like the best solution for a city that was separated into well-defined ethnic and racial communities. Shown here is a 1952 photo of Chicago Mayor Martin Kennelly (holding shovel) at a ground breaking ceremony for a high rise building on the city's far South Side. Eventually high-rise public housing in Chicago would prove to be a disaster. (Courtesy of City of Chicago: Graphics and Reproduction Center.)

A rare photo of Chicago's newly elected mayor Richard J. Daley (1955) at a groundbreaking ceremony for an extension to the Cabrini Green housing project complex northwest of the Loop. (Courtesy of City of Chicago: Graphics and Reproduction Center.)

This photo from the mid-1950s shows new housing built in the 1400 block of South Racine Avenue, southwest of the Loop. Efforts like the Racine project and others (both public and private) proved inadequate to meet the post-war needs. (Courtesy of City of Chicago: Graphics and Reproduction Center.)

Urban Growth

High-rise building construction in Chicago had been frozen by the Great Depression of the 1930s and limits imposed by World War II in the 1940s. The construction of the Prudential Building in 1954–55 broke the construction freeze and set off the building of a number of new high rises which shapes the modern Chicago skyline which includes one of the world's tallest buildings, the Sears Tower. (Courtesy of Chicago Assn. of Commerce/Industry.)

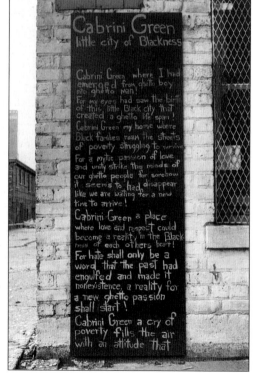

Black "Mural Art" often captured the residential and social changes occurring in public housing. Construction of Cabrini Green began in the early 1940s and residential preference was given to defense plant workers and U.S. servicemen. Southern blacks moved into the area increasingly during and after World War II, finding employment in the stockyards, steel mills, and defense industry. (Courtesy of G. Osofsky Collection.)

Black Chicago

Featured in this 1942 picture is Oscar DePriest (center), Chicago's first black alderman, who became the first 20th-century African American to hold a seat in Congress. He served from 1928 to 1935 as the New Deal's "Black Democrat." (Courtesy of Urban Historical Collection.)

Chicago's Negro Union Giants baseball team was a prominent member of the National Negro League. This league reached the height of its popularity in the mid-1940s when Chicago's Comiskey black East-West All-star Game drew more than 50,000 spectators. (Courtesy of Golda Mier Library Special Collection Milwaukee.)

African-American migrant workers agitated to lift the job ceiling, which both the labor shortages and the War Labor Board helped to lift to some extent. (Courtesy of Chicago Civil Defense Collection.)

Black migration to Chicago during World War II brought about some upward improvement in living standards, even though discrimination continued. Here, well-dressed African-American children can be seen buying tickets at a movie theater. (Courtesy of Urban Historical Collection.)

African-American migration from the South to Chicago picked up during World War II with the newcomers filling the job shortages caused by the war. With very little new housing construction done, the new migrants were often forced to move into crowded apartment buildings where families often doubled up. (Courtesy of UIC Special Collections.)

This photograph shows one of the first black families (Mr. and Mrs. Donald Howard and children) that moved into the Trumbull Park Housing Project in 1954. (Courtesy of Chicago Urban League Collection.)

This is a photo of one of the earliest civil rights protests in post-World War II Chicago, March 1954. Over 400 mainly African-American marchers picketed Chicago's City Hall protesting the violence at the Trumbull Park housing project on the city's far South Side. (Courtesy of Chicago Urban League Collection.)

Business

Founded in 1848, the Chicago Board of Trade had become the world's largest center for classifying, buying, and selling grain. Pictured above are Chicago Mayor Kennelly and the board officials celebrating the 1948 CBOT centennial. (Courtesy of Kennelly Collection.)

Founded in 1848, the Chicago Board of Trade set quality standards on grains and became the nation's trader in grains, agricultural goods, and later, other futures and commodities. By 1948 when it celebrated its one-century anniversary, the board's quality standards and pricing had become global. (Courtesy of Kennelly Collection.)

The opening of new retail stores and businesses was an important part of Chicago's post-war development. Some of the new retailers were a response to pent-up demand created by wartime rationing and shortage of consumer goods. On October 4, 1948, Chicago's mayor presided with company president R.C. Rolfing over the opening of a new Wurlitzer retail store on Wabash Avenue. (Courtesy of Kennelly Collection.)

Mayor Kennelly buying first ticket to the First United States International Trade Fair, August 7 to 20, from Adriana Carbonetti of Rome and his sister, Beatrice, children of Franco Carbonetti, Commercial Attache of the Italian Embassy. 1950.

Mayor Martin Kennelly buys the first ticket to the first United States International Trade Fair from Adriane Carbonetti of Rome (one and a half years old), and his sister Beatrice (age four) who were visiting Chicago for the Trade Fair with their father, Franco Carbonetti, commercial attaché of the Italian Embassy. The fair, held at Navy Pier and the International Ampitheater in August of 1950, displayed products from 47 different nations. (Courtesy of Kennelly Collection.)

Post-war Chicago sought to become an international center for trade and commerce. Mayor Kennelly and Austrian officials can be seen above opening up the Austrian exhibit booth at the 1950 International Trade Fair held in the Windy City. (Courtesy of Kennelly Collection.)

Politics

Joseph L. Gill   Col. J. Arvey   Mayor Kennelly

Mayor Kennelly (standing) is pictured at a Democratic party gathering in October 1947 with Joseph L. Gill (left) and Col. Jacob Avery (center). Avery was one of the nation's most powerful and influential big-city Democratic Party bosses. (Courtesy of Kennelly Collection.)

Wartime, Chicago Mayor Edward J. Kelly (far right) was prevented by Chicago Democratic leaders from seeking another term in 1947. This picture shows Mayor Kelly at a city council farewell dinner for him held at the Blackstone Hotel. Also, in the photo is Judge Roger Kiley (sitting) and City Controller R.B. Upham, and Cook County Democratic Party Chairman Jacob Arvey (standing). Arvey was the main architect of the Kelly dumping. (Courtesy of *Chicago Sun-Times*, April 1947.)

From left to right, Col. Jacob Arvey, a powerful ward boss, councilman, and Cook County Democratic Party chairman, celebrates his birthday on November 3, 1948 with Mayor Kennelly, Senator Scoot Lucas, ex-mayor Edward Kelly, and Judge Joseph Gill. Arvey was known as one of the most powerful urban ward bosses in America during the 1940s. (Courtesy of Kennelly Collection.)

Chicago Mayor Kennelly would give a radio talk in the 1940s on WBBM to communicate with the public. Chicago mayors adopted a routine established in the 1930s by two important East Coast leaders—President Franklin Roosevelt in his "fireside chats" and New York Mayor Fiorello LaGuardia's political chats. (Courtesy of Kennelly Collection.)

Mayor Martin Kennelly, seated on the right, celebrated former Alderman Charles Merriam's 75th birthday in 1949. Standing on the left is his son, Alderman Robert Merriam, who became a mayoral candidate in 1955 opposing Richard J. Daley; in the middle is Judge Otto Kerner, the father of a future governor of Illinois. (Courtesy of Kennelly Collection.)

The 20th anniversary annual meeting of the United States Conference of Mayors was held at the Waldorf Astoria in New York City. Shown being handed the gavel from the outgoing president Mayor David L. Lawrence is Mayor Martin H. Kennelly of Chicago, the newly elected president. (Courtesy of Kennelly Collection.)

At the Chicago Bears vs. Green Bay Packers football game, October 15, 1950 Mayor Kennelly welcomes Jim Swiatek, Mascot for the Bears. (Courtesy of Kennelly Collection.)

Pictured, from left to right, are Chicago alderman C. Weber, Mayor Richard J. Daley, and Councilmen Mathias "Paddy" Bauler. Bauler, who served 30 years after his 1933 election, is best known for his comment after Richard Daley's election in 1955 that "Chicago ain't ready for reform." (Courtesy of P. Bauler file, Urban Historical Collection..)

One of the nation's most frequent contenders for a presidential nomination, Harold Stassen socializes with Chicago Mayor Kennelly at a Board of Trade banquet on April 3, 1948. (Courtesy of Kennelly Collection.)

Mathias Paddy Bauler (left), a 43rd ward alderman who served in Chicago's City Council from 1933 to 1967, having lost one election in 1943, is seen here in the late 1940s with President Harry Truman. Bauler, a political machine Democrat, is most often quoted for saying, in 1955 when Richard J. Daley was first elected mayor, "Chicago ain't ready for reform." (Courtesy of Urban Historical Collection.)

Sales Executives Club of Chicago Rally
Held April 24, 1953

Former Vice President of the U.S.A.
Alben W. Barkley

Mayor Martin H. Kennelly

Chicago was a city that attracted not only American political leaders and governmental officials but also leaders from foreign nations. Former Vice President Alben Barkley is seen above socializing with Mayor Kennelly. (Courtesy of Kennelly Collection.)

The Chicago Council on Foreign Relations became an important agency in helping to internationalize and globalize a city which had been a center of isolationism and non-intervention before World War II. Above, Mayor Kennelly (left) meets U.S. Secretary of State George C. Marshall at a council banquet on November 18, 1947, at a time when the Marshall Plan to aid war-torn Europe was being put into effect. (Courtesy of Kennelly Collection.)

Illinois Governor Dwight Green (far left), Bishop Cardinal Stritch, and Chicago Mayor Kennelly greet Eamon De Valera, who became the Irish Free State President in 1932, at a formal dinner. (Courtesy of Kennelly Collection.)

Chicago's Irish Fellowship Dinner, March 20, 1948, saw Irish nationalist and one-time President of the Irish Free State, Eamon De Valera shaking hands with Mayor Martin Kennelly, a Chicagoan of Irish ancestry. All but three of Chicago's mayors from 1933 to the end of the century were of Irish ancestry. (Courtesy of Kennelly Collection.)

In May 1953, Chicago Mayor Kennelly welcomed Germany's Chancellor Dr. Konrad Adenauer to Chicago. Adenauer would later preside over the German "economic miracle" brought about by the adoption of the American free market system of which Chicago was a good example. (Courtesy of Kennelly Collection.)

Mayor Martin H. Kennelly and Chancellor Dr. Konrad Adenauer
May, 1953

Germany's Chancellor Konrad Adenauer comes to Chicago to meet Mayor Martin Kennelly and city leaders. (Courtesy of Kennelly Collection.)

Consul General of the Philippines, Leopoldo Ruiz making his first official call to Chicago. (Courtesy of Kennelly Collection.)

Consul General of the Republic Philippines Leopoldo T. Ruiz, his first official call on Mayor

Ethiopian Emperor Haile Selassie is welcomed by Mayor Kennelly during the summer of 1954. (Courtesy of Ethnic file, Urban Historical Collection.)

115

Mayor Kennelly welcoming Sheila Sheppard, British War Orphan, to Chicago. December, 1947

British war orphan Sheila Sheppard is welcomed to Chicago in December, 1947 by the Mayor. (Courtesy of Kennelly Collection.)

Baby Boom Age

The impact of the post-war baby boom generation hit Chicago like all other major American cities. Shown here is a street scene at 55th and Dorchester in the South Side Hyde Park neighborhood. (Courtesy of City of Chicago: Graphics and Reproduction Center.)

In 1951, Chicago's population peaked at 3,618,500. Post-war demands for more public services, especially public safety, accelerated with this increased growth. Shown here is a 1951 South Side fire being put out by the city's fire department with pre-war equipment. (Courtesy of City of Chicago: Graphics and Reproduction Center.)

This is an early 1950s photo of the bustling intersection 55th and Halsted on the city's South Side. Always known as the "City of Neighborhoods," Chicagoans would often identify themselves with their city council ward number, their catholic parish name, or the chief intersection running through their community. (Courtesy of City of Chicago: Graphics and Reproduction Center.)

This is an early 1950s overview of the north river area. This prime area north of the Loop went under utilized and undeveloped for many decades. Notice the open-air parking lot taking up valuable space for very few automobiles. It also clearly depicts transportation and manufacturing activities taking place north of the river. By the end of the 20th century, River North would transform itself into a high end residential and entertainment center. (Courtesy of City of Chicago: Graphics and Reproduction Center.)

Not all older housing in Chicago was in poor shape. This East 55th Street building in the University of Chicago Hyde Park neighborhood looks strong and sturdy as its owners attempt to upgrade the edifice to meet growing renter demand. (Courtesy of City of Chicago: Graphics and Reproduction Center.)

In the beginning of 1948, Chicago still had some 4,500 gas and gasoline lit street lamps. By the end of the year, some 3,500 gas and gasoline lamps had been replaced by electric streetlights. Above is Alderman Mathias Paddy Bauler directing the installation of new electric street lights in his North Side ward. (Courtesy of Bauler file, Kennelly Collection.)

Under Chicago's new mayor Richard J. Daley, making the city work was the order of the day. Here a new street cleaning machine is seen tidying up a Northwest Side Chicago neighborhood. (Courtesy of City of Chicago: Graphics and Reproduction Center.)

POSTSCRIPT

Chicago: 1955–2003

The emotional war and post-war era ended in 1955. In that year, Chicago elected a new mayor—Richard J. Daley (RJD). Mr. Daley would go on to serve 21 years, winning six mayoral general elections and two hotly contested Democratic mayoral primaries.

Few mayors have ever left a larger footprint on their city. RJD was known as "The Mayor," "Hizzoner," "The Boss," or simply "Mayordaley" (one word). And, though much has been written about this controversial and charismatic leader, one thing is seldom mentioned; he was the main force pushing Chicago into a new era of development. Under RJD's leadership Chicago would grow, prosper, and build—unfortunately at the same time the city and RJD would come face to face with the issue of race—an issue even the master politician could not overcome.

Key to understanding Chicago and for that matter RJD, is to examine the population surges and shifts that impacted Chicago during the last half of the 20th century. In 1950, Chicago's population peaked at 3.6 million people and equally important it made up 42 percent of all Illinois residents. From this mid-century high-water mark, Chicago lost people in every census until 2000 when its numbers grew by a little over 100,000 (2.9 million total—which gave the city less than a quarter of the state's population).

In the 1950s, Chicago was predominantly white, ethnic, and Catholic—a demographic that complemented RJD's personality, outlook, and philosophy. In every subsequent census Chicago's demographic changed, as first large numbers of African-Americans and later Hispanics migrated into the city—changing not only Chicago's complexion but also its politics.

Chicago's 2000 census reveals a city without a racial majority. Today's Chicago is 36 percent African-American, 31 percent Caucasian, and 26 percent Hispanic. Not only has there been major demographic shifting in the last 50 years, but also the city has seen radical rearrangements in its neighborhoods, commerce, and industry. Tourism and conventions as opposed to manufacturing now guide the city's economic fortunes. Even the often maligned but governmentally crucial Chicago City Council (by law Chicago has a weak mayor/strong council form of government) has a non-white majority, an inconceivable possibility to almost any Chicagoan in 1950.

One thing has not changed—the person running city government is a Daley—Mayor Richard M. Daley (RMD)—the son of RJD. How this phenomenon of Daley to Daley has occurred is without question the top story of Chicago's last half-century.

RJD became Cook County Democratic Party chairman in 1953 and two years later he became mayor. He inherited a faltering political organization or machine that had been put in place by former mayor Anton Cermak in 1931. RJD institutionalized Cermak's model of intertwining governmental and political activities. In fact, he moved from being another political boss to becoming a political legend because he was able to run his party and his city as a local service dispensing ward organization.

Like a strong ward committeeman, RJD did not share power. Instead, he personalized his governmental and political leadership—you were either "with him or against him"—and "him" to RJD was the city of Chicago and the Democratic Party organization. Unlike most American mayors past and present, RJD never shirked or avoided political or governmental responsibility. He was the mayor!

RJD's favorite slogan "good government is good politics and good politics is good government" moved Chicago into the forefront of American cities. The mayor imported bright young people to run his city, incredibly he convinced Chicagoans that "machine driven politics" would provide them with the best possible services—indeed he even borrowed the phrase "the city that works" to push his agenda.

To be sure RJD was not an exponent of town hall democracy. The older he became the less willing he was to listen to alternative views or, for that matter, new ideas. But at the outset of his six terms, this man from a working class neighborhood set an incredible pace for his city. Governmentally, he limited the city council's role in running or for that manner blocking his Chicago agenda. Politically, he was the only political boss to incorporate newly arriving blacks from the south into his organization. To be sure, racial issues would eventually dominate his last years in office and tarnish his reputation to outside observers—but let it not be forgotten that it was support from Chicago's African-American community that gave RJD victories in his original 1955 competitive contests and in his close 1963 re-election.

RJD gave Chicago O'Hare airport, new expressways, a downtown building boom, and most importantly, a sense of security. The 1968 Democratic National Convention and two major riots rattled many Chicagoans including RJD. Even though he carried every ward in his last campaign (1975)—it was clear to many his time had past. His death on December 20, 1976 signaled an end of an extraordinary era in the city.

The period from 1977 to 1989, described by some as the "Daley interregnum," produced the wildest politics in Chicago's history. Often unnoticed in this clash between the pursuit of power and racial politics was how the city was changing. The union stockyards, huge steel mills, center and peripheral city manufacturing areas were downsizing or simply disappearing. Chicago, like the rest of urban America during the 1980s was viewed by some as doomed. The Sunbelt and the suburbs were stealing urban jobs and people, while big cities like Chicago struggled to remain solvent and viable.

In 1979, Chicago elected its first and only female mayor—Jane Byrne. Her long-shot primary victory over Michael Bilandic (RJD's successor) was the first intra-party mayoral challenge lost by the city's regular Democratic organization since 1911.

To say her term was tumultuous was like saying hurricanes are windy. Mayor Byrne gave Chicago four years of gutsy, chaotic, and unpredictable political leadership. On one hand, she took on and beat entrenched public employee unions and promoted innovative plans for O'Hare expansion and downtown restoration and revitalization. Unfortunately, she also was incapable of developing a stable style of leadership and at times went out of her way to seek confrontation.

In 1983, Mayor Byrne was challenged by Congressman Harold Washington and Cook County States Attorney Richard M. Daley (RMD) in the Democratic mayoral primary. Without question this campaign was the "MAMP" (mother of all mayoral primaries). When the votes and dollars had settled, Mr. Washington had won a narrow victory over his two better-financed rivals. Five weeks later in a racially charged campaign, Chicagoans elected Mr. Washington over State Rep. Bernard Epton in the "MAME" (mother of all mayoral elections).

Never in the city's history had more dollars, energy, emotions, anger, fear, and pride mixed with campaign politics to produce two attention getting, high-turnout elections. In the end, Chicagoans elected its first African-American mayor—Harold Washington.

Mayor Washington's first term featured "Council Wars," as the aldermen divided primarily on racial lines to fight over the city's direction. Again the "shock and awe" of these spectacular race base struggles overshadowed the lingering problems of the city in the areas of employment, housing, crime, education, and economic development. Never in the city's history had such dynamic personalities commanded the political stage as rhetoric often ranged from heated to combustible.

Council Wars ended in early summer 1986 when Mayor Washington was able to take over the city council and its committees. A slight cooling of racial tensions lasted until November 1987 when the mayor, early into his second term, suddenly died and chaos and recrimination quickly returned to Chicago's political scene.

Eugene Sawyer, an African-American alderman, was selected interim mayor in a raucous all-night city council session that was combination vaudeville show and near urban riot. Mayor Sawyer lasted only 17 months due to a huge split in the black community. Many Mayor Washington loyalists refused to accept Mr. Sawyer and threw their support to another black alderman, Tim Evans, and moreover, they went to court with a lawsuit demanding a special mayoral election in early 1989. The Evansites won that battle, but undeniably lost the war. To say the least, this legal action was a huge mistake for Chicago's African-American community! Why? The sole benefactor of all the intra-black political fighting and court action was Cook County States Attorney Richard M. Daley. Like a professional poker player, RMD held his cards close to his chest, but when it came time to show his hand, he threw down nothing but aces.

RMD easily beat Mayor Sawyer in the 1989 special mayoral primary and Alderman Evans in the general election. Key to his victory, besides black disunity, was RMD's acceptance of the old political adage "you win elections by addition." Almost immediately, he and his shrewd advisors, aided by a huge campaign war chest, put together an unbeatable electoral coalition of white ethnics, Hispanics, and lakefront independents. Since 1989, RMD has breezed through four straight re-election campaigns and in the process has cooled the city's once red-hot politics.

Unlike his father, RMD has not gone the party route to achieve political control. His power is more personal and not institutional. He does not go to ward meetings, play a dominant role in top to bottom elective office slate making, or demand to become party chairman. Instead, he involves himself in selected political races while maintaining near total governmental control over all city functions through his role as "The Mayor." However, there are some striking similarities between RMD and RJD.

Like his father, he dominates his council through clever bargaining, fundraising, and if needed "raw power." Besides city government, RMD also controls the Chicago Board of Education and the Chicago Housing Authority. The takeover of these two huge bureaucracies was not done by stealth or backroom deals, rather it was simply handed to him, by state and federal officials who viewed RMD as a "can do manager." Cynics also suggested at the time that they simply dumped these two high profile governmental entities on RMD because they had become unmanageable.

Like his father, RMD's personal life, work ethic, and city boosterism is without blemish, but like his dad his mayoral longevity, his loyalty to friends, and at times meteoric temper has created some (not much) media criticism against his governing style. As of this writing, RMD's power is almost absolute in the city he loves and it exceeds the control of RJD at the height of his 21 years in office.

Chicago is "Daleyland." RMD's influence stretches from the public to the private sector, and it includes strategically placed Daley loyalists in almost every aspect of Chicago's economy. Added to this is RMD's capability to award "pinstripe patronage" (government contracts) to professional consultants, political supporters, and potential allies in the business world, and one can see the expansiveness of the mayor's power.

Lastly, RMD is careful in making sure his largesse is spread throughout the city (critics would argue unevenly) and since his decisions are seldom challenged, many minority businesses, churches, and community organizations have also received significant Daley rewards. It is important to stress again that all of this power comes from RMD as mayor and not the party leader, thus again separating himself from the old-style political party patronage dispensed by his father. To simplify the above analysis, take the word of a long-time Chicago political operative who said the main difference between RJD and RMD is that the latter believes "one generous contribution from a developer is more valuable than four garbage truck jobs."

All is not sunshine in RMD's Chicago. The mayor is perpetually on the prowl for more revenue. His city not only no longer dominates the state in population, it is constantly vying with its fellow Illinois cities and towns for businesses and jobs.

A disproportionate number of the state's tax takers (those receiving more in services than they pay in taxes) live in Chicago. RMD sees gentrification as a way to bring back or keep taxpayers (those who pay more in taxes than they receive in services) in his city, but by itself it is not enough. In recent years, former poor and working class near central city neighborhoods have become rejuvenated and expensive housing destinations. Signs of gentrification are popping up not only among Starbuck-drinking, cute restaurant-eating, and flower-buying yuppies and baby boomer returnees, but in minority communities as well. Many African-American and Hispanic aldermen cry for more market rate, as opposed to affordable housing, as their voters want to see their property values jump up like the rest of the city. However, for RMD, though neighborhood gentrification and rejuvenation are politically and economically beneficial (one of the reasons he won all 50 wards in his 2003 re-election campaign), they alone cannot produce the revenue needed to run the city.

In sum, Chicago in 2003 is a far less independent player in the state and national arenas than it was in 1955. It cannot generate enough dollars on its own to fund its infrastructure or social needs. In short, clout (the power to get things done) has moved south to Springfield (state capitol) and east to Washington, DC.

To be sure, Mayor Daley rules supreme within his city boundaries and due to this control can cut a wide path in the Illinois General Assembly or Congress. But he and Chicago need allies. It truly is not in his or the city's interest for RMD to be labeled "Mr. Democrat"—a title his dad wore proudly for decades. Instead, RMD would probably like to be known as "Mr. Revenue"— because no matter which party controls the state or national government, no matter if he is dealing with business or labor, no matter if he is negotiating with whites, blacks, or Hispanics, and no matter if he is pushing regional urban/suburban needs through a metropolitan caucus, RMD must constantly find new dollars to keep Chicago working.

Add to this revenue fixation, his control of schools and public housing in the city, public safety concerns (especially crime), and the myriad of traditional mayoral duties in a far more diverse city, and it becomes clear—running Chicago has grown more complicated and has changed greatly since the end of the post-war era.

Only one fact truly remains unchanged, neither Chicago baseball teams have won a world series in almost a century.

Bibliography

Barrett, Paul, *The Automobile and Urban Transit: Public Policy in Chicago* (Philadelphia: Temple Press, 1983).

Biles, Roger, *Big City Boss in Depression and War: Mayor Edward Kelly* (DeKalb, IL: Northern Illinois University Press, 1984).

Biles, Roger, *Richard J. Daley: Politics, Race, and the Governing of Chicago* (DeKalb, IL: Northern Illinois University Press, 1995).

Bukowski, Douglas, *"Big Bill" Thompson and the Politics of Image* (Urbana: University of Illinois Press, 1998).

Cohen, Adam and Taylor, Elizabeth, *American Pharaoh: Mayor Richard J. Daley* (Boston: Little Brown and Co. 2000).

Condit, Carl, *Chicago, 1930–70: Building, Planning and Urban Technology* (Chicago: University of Chicago Press, 1974).

Cutler, Irving, *Chicago Metropolis of the Mid-Continent* (Dubuque, IA: Kendall Hunt, 1982).

Duis, Perry, "Soldiers Without Guns," *Chicago History* XVI no. 3, Fall/Winter, 1987–88, 4–27.

Greeley, Andrew, *Neighborhood* (New York: Seabury Press, 1977).

Green, Paul M., *Paul Green's Chicago* (Springfield, IL: Illinois Issues, 1988).

Green, Paul M. and Holli, Melvin G., *Restoration: Chicago Elects a New Daley* (Chicago: Lyceum Books, 1991).

Green, Paul M. and Holli, Melvin G., eds. *The Mayors: The Chicago Political Tradition* (Carbondale, IL: Southern Illinois University Press, 1995).

Grimshaw, William, *Bitter Fruit: Black Politics and the Chicago Machine* (Chicago: University of Chicago Press, 1991).

Grossman, James R., *Land of Hope Chicago, Black Southerners, and the Great Migration* (Chicago: University of Chicago Press, 1989).

Heise, Kenan, *A Sampling of Chicago in the 20th Century: Chaos, Creativity, and Culture* (Salt Lake City: Gibbs, Smith Publisher, 1998).

Hirsch, Arnold, *Making the Second Ghetto: Race and Housing in Chicago*, 1940–1960 (New York: Cambridge Press, 1984).

Holli, Melvin G. and Green, Paul M., *A View From City Hall: Mid-Century to Millennium* (Charleston, SC: Arcadia Publishing, 1999).

Holli, Melvin G. and Jones, Peter d'A, *Ethnic Chicago: A Multicultural Portrait* (Grand Rapids, MI: Eerdmans Publishing, 1995).

Holli, Melvin G. and Green, Paul M., *The Making of the Mayor: Chicago 1983* (Grand Rapids, MI: Eerdmans Publishing, 1984).

Holli, Melvin G. and Green, Paul M., *Bashing Chicago Traditions: Harold Washington's Last Campaign* (Grand Rapids, MI: Eerdmans Publishing, 1989).

Kennedy, Eugene, *St. Patrick's Day with Mayor Daley* (New York: Seabury Press, 1976).

Mayer, Harold Mayer and Wade, Richard C., *Chicago: Growth of a Metropolis* (Chicago: University of Chicago Press, 1969).

Miller, Donald, *City of the Century: The Epic of Chicago* (New York: Simon Schuster, 1996).

Nelli, Humbert, *The Italians in Chicago: A Study in Ethnic Mobility* (New York: Oxford Press, 1970).

Pacyga, Dominic and Skerrett, Ellen, *Chicago: City of Neighborhoods* (Chicago: Loyola University Press, 1986).

Platt, Harold, *The Electric City: Energy and the Growth of the Chicago Area, 1880–1930* (Chicago: University of Chicago Press, 1991).

Rakove, Milton, *Don't Make No Waves: Don't Back no Losers: An Insiders Analysis of the Daley Machine* (Bloomington, IN: Indiana University Press, 1975).

Simpson, Dick, *Rogues, Rebels, and Rubber Stamps* (Boulder, CO: Westview Press, 2001).

Sautter, R. Craig and Burke, Edward M., *Inside the Wigwam: Chicago Presidential Conventions, 1860–1996* (Chicago: Loyola Press, 1996).

Sawyers, June, *Chicago Portraits: Biographies of 250 Famous Chicagoans* (Chicago: Loyola Press, 1991).

Suttles, Gerald D., *The Man-Made City: Land Use Confidence Game in Chicago* (Chicago: University of Chicago Press, 1990).

Travis, Dempsey, *An Autobiography of Black Politics* (Chicago: Urban Research Press, 1987).

Waters, Mary, *Illinois in the Second World War, I, II* (Springfield, IL: Illinois State Historical Library, 1952).

Young, David, *Chicago Transit: An Illustrated History* (DeKalb, IL: Northern Illinois University Press, 1998).